Assurance Statement

"This report has been submitted to an independent assurance assessment carried out by The SROI Network. The report shows a good understanding of the SROI process and complies with SROI principles. Assurance here does not include verification of stakeholder engagement, data and calculations. It is a principles-based assessment of the final report".

Executive Summary

Caring for Adults with learning disabilities uses local government resources (money), and there are many other priorities for these limited resources. The money allocated to adults with learning disabilities will need to be used wisely to get the best possible results. The Care Quality Commission (CQC) has established a number of standards to make sure that organisations that provide care meet certain minimum levels. But the CQC standards only measure practical things, like "do the staff have the right training?", and "is the environment safe?"

> *"What would you want in YOUR home?"*
>
> Mike Maguire – Worcestershire Supporting People

People who receive support want to be able to live a full life, just like someone who does not require support. They want to have choices, they want to live in a nice place with people they like, and they want to spend time with people who they can respect, and who respect them. This "user experience" is much more difficult to measure.

Quality Checkers was established to understand how people with learning disabilities experience the service they receive. It was established by Skills for People (Newcastle upon Tyne, UK) in around 2005, and has trained Quality Checker teams throughout England. The Quality Checkers are people with learning disabilities, experts by experience, employed as professionals. The people they interview feel confident talking with a person who has the same "label" as them, which means they get to the truth. The experts by experience notice things that other people (without experience of receiving services) won't notice – things that may seem trivial but are actually very important.

> *"People think that staff do not listen to them when they complain"*
>
> Dawn McGreevy – South Tyneside Direct Services

Quality Checkers developed the REACH standards with Paradigm in 2006. The11 REACH standards are national standards for user experience which can be used to show if people are being supported properly.

We wanted to know about – Value for Money.

We wanted to find out if the Quality Checkers represent value for money. Quality Checkers need to be paid; they need to travel to do their audit, the audits take a lot of time, and the reports have to be written; and the people they interview have to be organised and supported. So is it all worth it? If you invite Quality Checkers in to do audits, do you get more value back than the amount you spend on the audits, or the training to give audits?

We found a way to ask the question.

An independent auditor spoke with the Quality Checkers, service provider organisations (residential and day care, support workers in people's own homes, housing agencies and advocacy groups), people who had been audited, and commissioners (typically the local authority) to ask what they thought.

I used semi-structured interview techniques, basing it on the Social Return on Investment (SROI) framework, which is a robust, internationally recognised way of working out what the benefits are, and calculating a financial equivalent of the benefits. It tells us when a service represents value for money, even though what you get from the service isn't usually measured in money terms (for example: choices, happiness).

With SROI, the people who get the benefits are the people who decide how much we should say it's are worth. With SROI, we ask at least two or three organisations for each group of stakeholders (for example, local authority social care departments, and people who get audited), so we can find out if the answers are about the same.

The groups of stakeholders were:

- People receiving support who had audits

- Quality Checker Trainees

- Organisations which provide social care services

- Similar organisations and competitors

- Regulators, policy advisors, other advocacy groups

- Commissioners of services

I asked them about the services they had received in the last 2 ½ years (April 2008 to October 2010), because they could still remember what had happened, and also it was long enough to see some of the longer-term benefits.

We looked at what they said

The Quality Checkers submit their report at the end of their audit. The Quality Checkers already know what their reports recommend and can see what a difference their report could make. But they haven't had a chance to go back and see whether the home or support workers have made the changes, and whether it has made a big difference. When I interviewed people and organisations, I found there had been a chain reaction; as people gained confidence and experience. The people we asked told us that:

- people were inspired when they met the Quality Checkers, and realised that they are no longer powerless, they can find paid employment as professionals with specific skills

- people said what they really think, because they knew they were being listened to; this means that the managers knew what needed to change, so they could put things right before it became expensive

- the staff learned that they are not there to wrap people in cotton wool, but to help them live a full and rich life, with choices and risks

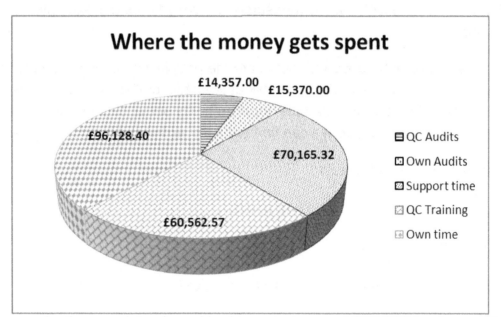

Where the money gets spent

£14,357.00
£15,370.00
£96,128.40
£70,165.32
£60,562.57

- QC Audits
- Own Audits
- Support time
- QC Training
- Own time

The organisations we interviewed had invested around £90,000 buying audits and training (including audits by their own Quality Checkers teams) in the last two and half years (from April 2008 to October 2010), and around £70,000 on staff support during audits (ie staff supporting people to be at interviews, and staff attending the reporting sessions afterwards). The Quality Checker trainees had spent many hours of their own time attending courses, which was worth around £96,000 (based purely on the Disability Living Allowance – it worked out at £5.05 per hour). People who had audits didn't want to put a cost in for their time, because it was so important to them that they had the audits.

> *"if things are left unchecked, then what will the financial consequences be?"*
>
> Bob Tindall – United Response

The total investment in Quality Checkers' audits, training and everything else added up to £256,583, of which Skills for People's Quality Checkers were paid £74,919.

We found there are a lot of benefits, and some aren't obvious.

Following a Quality Checker audit, care and support can be delivered for lower cost because:

- staff understand the people they support better, and are happier, so they don't leave so quickly or take so much sick leave

- people feel they are being listened to, so they don't have to get frustrated or resort to challenging behaviour

- the managers can make changes people really want, instead of trying to guess and make expensive mistakes

- when the clients become part of the management team, they came up with interesting, better and often cheaper solutions

The SROI technique works out how much all of this is worth, and whether it really is the result of the Quality Checker audits. We found 26 benefits that we could show were a result of the audits.

The people I interviewed told me of the benefits they got, and working it out over a 5 year period using Present Value techniques, it came to nearly £3 million (£2,927,102). They also got benefits that we didn't put a value to.

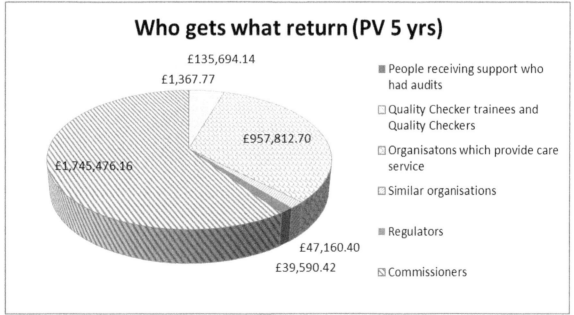

We then worked out an SROI ratio (Social Return on Investment ratio). The SROI ratio is the amount of benefit divided by the cost. For Quality Checkers service, this is around 11:1 (£3million divided by £260,000), which means that for every £1,000 spent on Quality Checkers (either training or audits), you get about £11,400 back in benefits.

This is an estimate based on what the people we interviewed told us. We worked out the maximum and the minimum that they told us, and the SROI ratio could be as little as 8.6, or as much as 18.

With these numbers, the Quality Checkers seem to offer real value for money. Many Quality Checker groups around the country are developing Health Quality Checkers, who say what it is like to use a particular health service, from the point of their own disability. On the basis of my interviews, I'd say that these will return a similar amount of benefit.

Acknowledgements

This report relies completely on the input of so many different people, from so many different organisations. The organisations are listed in the report, and I thank the effort of the people who gave of their time, their wisdom and their effort to provide the information to make up the report.

It could not have happened without Kathy Steele, Suzie and Anthony Fothergill, and Billy Richardson, the Quality Checkers from Newcastle and North Tyneside who run quality checks around England and Scotland – this report shows how much difference you make, and thank-you for your input. I'm grateful to Skills for People for making this happen.

Thank-you also to Tim Goodspeed who showed me what SROI is, to Sheila Durie who corrected my half-understood efforts and made a robust report, and Tania Vera-Burgos who kept on at me to complete the report in time for an assessment round.

Table of Contents

Who are Quality Checkers, and who uses them?

The Quality Checkers make a difference to people's lives, in so many subtle ways. I wanted to perform a full SROI evaluation in order to quantify the difference that they make.

This is about Skills for People - Quality Checkers and Health Quality Checkers

Skills for People is a charity and company limited by guarantee based in Newcastle upon Tyne. It provides services to disabled people, their families; and organisations which supply or commission services for disabled people. It develops and demonstrates new ways of improving the lives of disabled people, especially those with learning disabilities. Services include advocacy, training, awareness raising, consultancy, support for self advocacy and user involvement.

The Quality Checkers service was developed by Skills for People and delivers checks and training throughout the country. Quality Checkers specifically focusses on Independent Supported Living services (ISL) and supported living services which includes help for adults with learning disabilities to live in their own homes, or to live in shared accommodation but able to make their own choices and enjoy largely independent lives. The Quality Checkers service uses experts by experience[1] as paid auditors, to use their own experience of services to make checks of support services, and to give a view that is often missing from most quality reviews. Their work helps to make sure services truly support people with learning disabilities to live full and healthy lives. Supported living services for people with learning disabilities already have to meet high standards, such as safety, staff training, and being involved in your development plan(DH 2009). But these standards aren't able to measure their experience of the service.

The Quality Checkers service uses experts by experience as paid auditors, to make sure that people who receive support, get high quality support. Supported living services for people with learning disabilities already have to meet high standards, such as safety, staff training, and being involved in your development plan. But these standards aren't able to measure their experience of the service.

People who receive supported living services, whether this is a support worker in their own home, day-care services, or residential, often feel vulnerable and unconfident. When they receive an inspection, they will usually tell the visiting professional what they think that professional wants to hear, usually that the service is "fine". This is especially true when the visiting professional doesn't have time to let the person being interviewed get comfortable. It is even more difficult to complain

---

[1] Experts by Experience is a widely used term to refer to people who choose to help others in the same circumstances as themselves because of their own experience of those circumstances. It applies equally to Adults with Learning Disabilities receiving Supported Living services (in this case), people whose first language is not English who are applying for a passport, and of course 101 other situations.

when the care worker is present, and often a person receiving supported living services cannot complete a paper questionnaire on their own.

So the Valuing People program from the Department of Health commissioned Paradigm and Skills for People (with other organisations) to develop the REACH standards for people with learning disabilities in supported living. Skills for People developed a team of people (and training courses) for Quality Checkers who go to people's homes and speak to people who get support, carers and families, and staff to find out what it's like to live there and to make sure the REACH standards are being met.

"It's about people feeling comfortable, it's not a platform to have a grumble, and that's why the Quality Checkers report is so balanced"

Maxine Naismith, Assistant Director Social Care, Darlington MBC

The 11 REACH standards.

Standard 1 REACH
I choose who I live with

Standard 2 REACH
I choose where I live

Standard 3 REACH
I have my own home

Standard 4 REACH
I choose how I am supported

Standard 5 REACH
I choose who supports me

Standard 6 REACH
I get good support

Standard 7 REACH
I choose my friends and relationships

Standard 8 REACH
I choose how to be healthy and safe

Standard 9 REACH
I choose how I take part in my community

Standard 10 REACH
I have the same rights & responsibilities as other citizens

Standard 11 REACH
I get help to make changes in my life

Skills for People also offers training courses so that other people can become Quality Checkers, and make a difference where they are.

Most people who volunteer themselves to become Quality Checkers are adults with learning disabilities. The course teaches communication and assessment skills, and reinforces the national standards of care that the auditors should expect to find (REACH standards[2] which the Skills for People Quality Checkers helped to develop,

---

[2] Skills for People had developed a number of User Experience standards within their "It's My Home" programme which were user focussed, whereas Paradigm had developed nine user experience standards

or a local variation if required). When people do the exercises in the course (such as "You and I"), they understand what it all means.

> *"It's about meeting new people and teaching them about the service they should receive. There's a real sense of achievement when people write back saying that they found things themselves that we taught them to look for"*
>
> Anthony Fothergill, Quality Checker

Once people have completed the course, they will usually practice some more to reinforce key lessons before starting to run their own audits and writing their own final reports. Some organisations have used Skills for People to reinforce the training and update the skills annually or every 18 months.

The people who personally get most out of the Quality Checker audits are the people receiving support, and people who train as Quality Checkers. But lots of other people said that they got a lot out of the audits as well – staff and support workers, social care organisations, the regulators and Department of Health, and commissioners (typically local authority social services)[3].

What is Social Return on Investment (SROI)?

SROI is a way of understanding what benefits you get from a service. It identifies and records benefits like happiness, longer living, having more choices, as well as the kind of benefits that you can put a number against. SROI then tries to estimate a number to put against the benefits that are more difficult to measure.

SROI is based on seven key principles:

1. **Involve stakeholders**: instead of relying on the Quality Checkers to say how valuable they are themselves, I asked the people who benefit (the customers, people being audited, organisations audited) and to tell me what they think the benefits are, and how much they are worth.

2. **Understand what changes**: I asked about what difference the Quality Checkers made. Lots of things are changing all the time, and I want to know what is due to the Quality Checkers and what is happening anyway. I also

---

which were self-reported by the service provider. The current 11 REACH standards combine the two so they are reported and evaluated by people receiving support, carers, family and staff.

[3] I've used the term "Commissioners" throughout to refer to the organisations that actually procure the services and manage them. These organisations manage a budget proportional to a person's need, so if someone receiving supported living at the standard level, starts to exhibit "challenging" behaviour, then the Commissioners are responsible for increasing the budget and payments for this person. This subtle distinction will become very important during this report.

find out what is a good change (changes that makes things better) and what is a bad change (makes things worse).

3. **Value the things that matter**: many times people can tell us about something that changed for just one person, or something that is exciting to the person I'm interviewing, only it doesn't make much difference to the person who has to live with it. With SROI we try to measure things for the people who have to live with them; and we them to say how much it is worth to them.

4. **Only include what is material**: make sure that every benefit we include actually makes a difference. This means making sure that we include every negative consequence as well as every positive consequence, and understand what difference it makes. It also means leaving out things that aren't actually important to the stakeholders. We did this by asking people and checking and double-checking that everything we included is important.

5. **Do not over claim**: often lots of things change at once. SROI works out which things happened **BECAUSE OF** the change we're investigating, and what would happen anyway so we don't include it as a benefit. I've used a term Attribution to estimate how much of a change is due to the Quality Checkers – and again it is up to the person to decide, not up to me. We've also made sure we don't count things twice - when one leads to another you should only count the last one. With SROI, we are very careful about this.

6. **Be transparent**: everywhere I've used a number, I can show where it came from, and why I used it. I've also spoken to the person who gave me the number, to check I've used it correctly.   I've checked it against numbers from other people, to check that it makes sense.

7. **Verify the result**: Everything in this audit came from the people we interviewed, and they checked it, and checked each other's answers. They also looked at the whole report (twice), to make sure it makes sense.

What happens when you use Quality Checkers? What are we reporting on?

The Quality Checkers can do one of two things:

- They can either do an audit, in which case they go around interviewing the people who receive support, and their family and carers and staff, and write a report.

- Or they can put together a training course, and train a mixed group so that the experts by experience in that group can go off and become Quality Checkers themselves (or take any other employment).

I'll just show how this works with a couple of examples.

Gateshead MBC – training

Gateshead Learning Disability Partnership Board had already developed a set of standards in partnership with people with a learning disability and family carers. A team of people with a learning disability and family carers were recruited and trained as Quality Checkers. Skills for People delivered the training.

Gateshead particularly appreciated that the training was flexible enough to incorporate the standards they had developed, rather than only the REACH standards.

The way the training is delivered gives people the self-confidence to speak out. For the people, their families and carers, they came to trust that their views would be listened to and acted upon. They recognised that Gateshead's intention is that everyone has an opportunity to live a full life. The way Quality Checkers delivers the training gets underneath the layers of abstract, and really makes it practical and useful, and memorable, to the people on the course.

These confident people now form a Quality Checking team which supports the Learning Disability Partnership Board to ensure that services are of a good quality. They are confident to speak out and get their views heard, and they are aware enough to speak for everybody, rather than just for their own individual and particular interests.

Darlington MBC – audits

Darlington Council had a substantial "new opportunities" campus re-provisioning project in 2006, which also made the changes needed from the Turnbull judgement{Etchells, 2003 #1}(Turnbull 2006). An evaluation was commissioned in 2008, and the Quality Checkers were brought in as part of this evaluation, to see how campus re-provisioning had affected people receiving support.

Darlington Council particularly appreciated the work that the Quality Checkers put into preparations and meetings before beginning the audits. They involved all parties in workshops, especially the commissioners of the new services themselves. They made sure that everybody understood what they should expect from the Quality Checker audits – the audits aren't simply a confirmation that the campus re-provisioning project has gone well, but are a benchmark against national standards, using a nationally accepted method of evaluation.

The people involved in re-provisioning, and in delivering care and support, spoke especially highly of the Quality Checkers because of the way they contributed to the workshops during and immediately after their audits, before their report was complete. The Quality Checkers provided feedback (and supported people who had moved into independent supported living to provide feedback) in the right way, and at the right time, so that things that needed to be changed could be put right in a timely manner. People receiving support were able to speak up with confidence in these workshops, and hold their ground and justify their position when challenged.

Quality Checkers were quick to submit their final report. This was – thankfully – not just a transcription of a whole lot of interviews. The comments had been carefully put into context. Recommendations were made. It was relatively straightforward for the Council and the providers to take action on every point made, and perhaps more to the point, to take action at low cost, whilst achieving the best results for the recipient (whichever stakeholder group they represented).

Darlington had commissioned the whole campus re-provision evaluation from one organisation – Inclusion North – so they were not aware how much has been spent on Quality Checkers evaluation. They believe it represents excellent value for money, and they have much more confidence that the campus re-provision project did what it was supposed to do. Quality Checkers were able to tell me how much money they got paid by Inclusion North, so this is included in the Value For Money analysis.

South Tyneside Direct Services – audits

South Tyneside Council intend to develop their own Quality Checker team, and commissioned audits on two provider services to see how they work. They had originally intended to audit one in-house provided service and one external service; in the end they audited two in-house services because the timing made it difficult to select which external provider to review.

They were impressed with the amount of preparation that the Quality Checkers do before beginning audits. Before going in to talk to the residents, the Quality Checkers had already discussed how the service is currently provided, and they had run workshops with commissioners and providers to make sure everybody knew what was going to happen.

People receiving support were asked if they would like to take part, and of the 19 people in Danesfield, quite a number volunteered. They warmed to the Quality Checkers immediately, and felt that they could speak freely with them. Staff also felt very comfortable with having the Quality Checkers in the homes of the people they supported, which meant that the Quality Checkers had a chance to see what really went on. As a result, the Quality Checker audits recorded a wealth of accurate and complete information that the provider service could take action on.

Perhaps most importantly, the Quality Checkers wrote and presented their report extremely quickly. This meant that people recognised/remembered what they had said, or what they were doing at the time. The report meant something to them – usually, a report takes so long to come out that people can't remember what it was about and the services have changed.

The report was extremely high quality, highlighting a number of very good things that should be shared, some bad things that need correcting, and some staff attitudes that needed re-training before they became the norm. The provider service had recently recruited a large number of new staff, so it was very timely to identify poor staff attitudes.

Most of the things the Quality Checkers identified were put right immediately – but it was important that they were put right immediately, otherwise the situation could have got worse. One or two things, if left unchecked, could have become extremely damaging (and expensive) situations.

They said they would like the Quality Checkers to come back every two years to make sure that services are constantly improving – they found the exercise extremely valuable.

VoiceAbility (used to be called Advocacy Partners) – training

Surrey used to have the largest number of long-stay hospitals in Europe, so when campus re-provisioning began, Surrey had further to go. With this in mind, Advocacy Partners developed a tool to understand how people experienced services, which was similar to the way the Quality Checkers did audits. They needed to train nine self-advocates (experts by experience) to do the audits, and Skills for People's Quality Checkers were invited in to provide the training.

The Quality Checkers did a lot of preparation before the course, so that they could talk about real places and real people in Surrey and bring the course alive. It made a real difference to the people on the course, getting them engaged, inspired, and full of energy. After the course people understood and remembered what to do when they do a quality check.

> *"it helps us learn about what makes good support, and helped us gain confidence to do the job"*
>
> VoiceAbility trainee

For Advocacy Partners, there were some delays such as getting CRB checks. They did other kinds of training to keep the energy up, such as safeguarding training. People felt really good about having a real job, and everything that goes with having a job (social life, identity, purpose, pay).

The training also inspired people to want to do the job properly: "this is our project, and this is what we want to do" and "we meet people who are sad and unhappy when they speak. We help people to make changes".

Seven people work as Quality Checkers, receiving an hourly rate of £6.80, and the audits can be classed "permitted work" so they don't affect someone's disability benefits. One person also has a job as a travel trainer. Every person who received training says it has made a big difference in their life. They are more confident speaking up, they understand about working as a team, and they understand about other people's points of view.

> *"Quality Checkers is a proper job; you're working as a team for paid services"*
>
> VoiceAbility trainee

The people who received a Quality Checker audit have also benefited; Advocacy Partners' (now VoiceAbility) first quality check was in a residential care service where there were a number of concerns, one of which was about the social opportunities for people receiving support. The action plan has already made a difference – the service now offers a number of different activities and has an activities worker, and people are supported to get back in touch with old friends.

United Response – training

United Response engaged the Quality Checkers through the Association for Supported Living. Their initial interest was in the South West Division during 2008, and they use the audits to help inform their highly successful "Way We Work" organisational framework. Way We Work reviews have always made efforts to include the views of the people supported by United Response, and the Quality Checkers complement this in addition to their primary function of reporting on the quality of individual services.

Because of the scale of the requirement within United Response, they are training their own teams of Quality Checkers, who will be involved in around four audits per year each.

The first thing that United Response noticed, is that more of the people receiving support now feel that they have the right to speak up. They themselves have been listened to by a professional auditor, someone with a "label like them". The auditor has been listened to, and their recommendations have been acted upon. So the person now has the confidence to say what they want, when they want to, and to expect to be heard.

What does this mean? Well it certainly helps United Response's efforts to create an environment where it's OK to complain, to encourage people to speak up if there's something that they're not happy about, and then ensure that improvements are made to put things right. Many of the complaints (80%) are sorted out on the spot, by the local manager and staff team, and sorting out these problems costs very little. It can also provide an additional communication channel for those whose only way to communicate has been through their behaviour, which can often be referred to as 'challenging'. If people don't feel that they are being listened to or that enough effort is being made to understand what they are saying, then they often find other ways to make themselves heard, and this can mean increased costs because of the need for additional support hours.

United Response has always involved people they support in the organisation's management decisions. The Quality Checkers are able to contribute in an even better way. They can speak from personal experience, and back it up with examples from other people. They can decide what is a common problem, and what is rare or unique. They have much more confidence, to discuss their suggestions when challenged and to involve themselves in deciding what action should be taken. United Response has complemented its structure of divisional management teams to include Quality Checkers. Instead of being consulted, users of services now make the decisions.

> *"Quality Checkers influence the leadership meetings and influence the decisions made in those meetings. This means changing the priorities, for example, focusing on the things that matter to people we support (harassment, employment opportunities, bank accounts, staff in a bad mood at work). Change the priority from "yes that's the problem that needs fixing" to "something gets done"*
>
> Dave Glover/ Bob Tindall – United Response

Attitudes have changed amongst staff too. Staff have clear evidence that the people they support know what they want from their lives (many of United Response's customers communicate in ways that require staff to have specific skills). Staff are more closely matched (for example, to the goals in the development plan) to the people they support, and United Response can give the appropriate support for people to recruit their own support workers. United Response believes that this has affected staff retention, sickness/ absence, and improved staff attitudes.

Initially, United Response South West division showed that Quality Checkers work for adults with learning disabilities, and now the other divisions have also developed teams of Quality Checkers.

Scope of this evaluation

This SROI Evaluation looks at the work of the Quality Checkers at Skills for People in Newcastle, UK. We've chosen a representative period of two and a half years from April 2008 to October 2010 to obtain evaluation information, for three reasons:

1   because this is reasonably recent, so the methods and processes that the Quality Checkers use are mostly stable and aren't evolving as fast as they were when the Quality Checkers were new

2   some impacts take more than 12 months to show (I've based the evaluation on organisations and audits which happened during the representative period, so we need a longer evaluation period in order to measure and report changes that take longer than 12 months to become measurable), and

3   people can still remember the audits, what life was like before the audits, and what changed.

During this time, the Quality Checkers ran audits for 27 organisations and ran 18 training courses.

I've included within the evaluation the costs of training additional teams of Quality Checkers, together with the difference some of these additional teams have made. A number of teams have completed training but not yet started delivering audits, and part of the reason for this evaluation is to give them some evidence to approach the organisations and commissioners in their area to offer Quality Checker audits.

Theory of Change

Services for adults with learning disabilities have changed dramatically over the last few years, with campus re-provision (helping people out of institutions, and into supported living), and the Turnbull judgement(Turnbull 2006). Organisations that commission services for adults with learning disabilities, and organisations that provide those services, need to treat them as adults, to give them life choices, and support them to grow.

This is a tall order: staff may be used to the old way of doing things; organisations may still believe that their role is to keep people safe ("wrapped up in cotton wool"), rather than to let them take risks; organisations may think that involving users will be expensive and lead to expensive requests; change is always risky, and often resisted.

Commissioners and providers have always needed robust methods of getting feedback on the people they support, so they can understand what is good, and what needs to be changed.

The cheapest way is a paper questionnaire. Questionnaires are usually completed by the support worker, or with the support worker on hand to help, which limits the amount of criticism that the person receiving support will make. Very often, adults with learning disabilities have had a lifetime of being punished whenever they complain, so they are unlikely to criticise their support services, even when they are in an environment where anonymity is guaranteed. "It's us and them". Some organisations have developed user panels which they hoped would mean that the voice of the user would be heard. The results have been variable.

Quality Checkers approaches this from a different direction. Adults with learning disabilities feel comfortable talking to auditor with the same "disability" as themselves. In many cases, the adults with learning disabilities have exceptional people skills – empathy, the ability to get someone to talk, the ability to get to the root of the problem. Of course they also spot problems, based on their own experience of receiving supported living. So if you want to know what people think, then the best people to ask are people like them – the Quality Checkers.

> *"People think that staff do not listen to them when they complain"*
>
> Dawn McGreevy – South Tyneside Direct Services

Quality Checkers originally developed a set of standards that they can use to compare different services across the country, and that will improve the standard of service that everyone receives, from user experience point of view. These standards were called "It's My Home".

Paradigm, which is well-known for championing user experience, had also developed a set of REACH standards which could be answered by organisations. Using experts by experience to interview the recipients of services (the adults with learning disabilities who receive supported living services) is a much better way of finding out what people think, so Paradigm and Skills for People, along with a number of other organisations, developed the 11 REACH standards that are now used (REACH 2).

Quality Checkers deliver training for commissioners and provider organisations, and advocacy groups, so they can develop their own teams of Quality Checkers, to provide local audits that are to the national standards, and use the national method. Quality Checkers also audit services, and deliver recommendations and an action plan, to improve the user experience of the people receiving support.

These action plans help organisations to do what they are required by law, to improve user experience. Of course this is important. But the biggest impact of the Quality Checkers comes about because of how they do it (rather than what they do).

The biggest impact is on the people receiving support, and the staff who support them. As I recorded above, adults with learning disabilities often feel vulnerable when talking to someone in uniform or a suit. The Quality Checker auditor is someone they can immediately relate to, and have confidence in. The interviews are structured, so they talk about the things they like, and the things they don't like, and manage to say everything they want to say. They have time to talk, whereas a professional auditor may only have a couple of hours to audit a whole organisation.

The Quality Checker report is tangible evidence that they have been listened to, and when the action plan changes their home, or their day centre, then they know that their views have been listened to. They no longer need to resort to other ways to get themselves noticed; they can speak up and describe their needs and wants. As they gain confidence, they demand more choices, but this seems to cost less overall (according to the stakeholder views documented here).

For staff, much the same transformation occurs. Quality Checkers talk to staff as well as users and carers. They use a national set of standards (the REACH standards, listed above), and they use a nationally accepted standard way of performing audits. When the commissioner or the management team say that care has to be delivered in a certain way, staff know that it can be measured, and that they can do really well or miss the required standard.

They recognise that the people they support do actually have their own opinions, and instead of wanting to be kept safe, they want to take risks like everyone else. In some places, these small changes have meant the staff are much more satisfied, both emotionally and professionally, at work. Staff enjoy feeling that they are making a difference to someone's life, instead of just keeping someone safe. Staff costs have actually gone down, as sickness/absence reduces, as retention improves, as complaints about staff and consequent disciplinary action have reduced. The REACH standards are a necessary foundation, an enabler. But according to our stakeholders involved in this study, the real difference is through using other adults with learning disabilities as paid professional auditors.

A list of people we spoke to, and why we chose them

The independent auditor held a workshop with the Quality Checkers at Skills for People to discover who the main stakeholder groups were. We talked about who benefited, who contributed, and who else might be interested.

Analysis of stakeholders and stakeholder groups

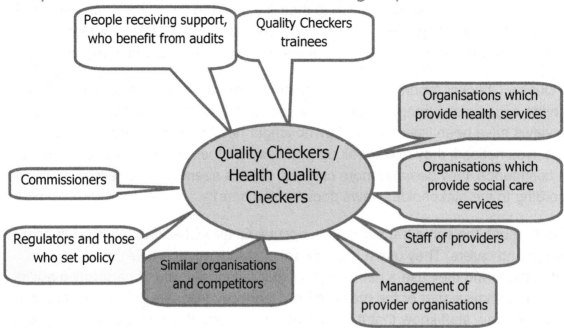

The main beneficiaries are the groups above and to the right. They comprise the individuals who receive audits and their families and carers, and people trained as Quality Checkers who may get jobs; and the organisations and their staff which provide services.

Another key group who benefit are commissioners of services (to the left), especially statutory commissioners.

> "I never dreamt that I would go on a Board or speak in front of hundreds of people. We are learning all the time. People have been listened to. I used to be a person that nobody thought could do anything, but now I'm going all over the country! People look at us and say 'I could do that'."
>
> Suzie Fothergill, Quality Checker

Regulators and policy advisors (also to the left) don't have much to gain but are a key stakeholder, and similar organisations (below, grey background) were difficult to identify since the organisations which use a similar model have (mostly) been trained by the Quality Checkers and so fall into the category of Quality Checkers trainees.

The organisations and people interviewed are listed below (clockwise around the above diagram – some organisations have more than one role):

- Organisations representing People receiving support who receive audits
    - Renaissance Social Housing
    - United Response
    - Advance UK
    - South Tyneside direct services

- People receiving audits
  - People supported by South Tyneside direct services, interviewed as a group
- QC trainees
  - Suzie, Billy and Anthony at Skills for People
  - A family member
  - Sharon, Rachel and Sheila at Sunderland People First
- Organisations representing QC trainees
  - United Response
  - Advance UK
  - Worcestershire Supporting People
  - Poole Forum
  - Sunderland People First
- Providers of services which are audited – social care
  - United Response
  - Advance UK
  - South Tyneside direct services
  - Gateshead Council
  - Barnsley direct services
- Staff of providers who change their attitudes (staff at all of the following)
  - United Response
  - Advance UK
  - South Tyneside direct services
- Provider management who experience a tangibly different culture amongst staff
  - United Response
  - Advance UK
- Commissioners able to commission improved services because of Quality Checker audits
  - North Tyneside Learning Disability Partnership Board
  - Worcestershire Supporting People
  - Gateshead MBC
  - Darlington MBC
  - North East SHA
- Policy makers, policy advisors, Regulators
  - Department of Health 'Valuing People Now' Policy Lead – North-East
  - Inclusion North
  - North East SHA
  - Care Quality Commission (CQC)
- Advisors, often Peers and other Advocacy Groups (including competitors)
  - Both Ways (Worcestershire – part of OurWay)
  - Enough is Enough
  - Sunderland People First
  - Poole Forum

o   VoiceAbility

Because of the nature of the audit, it was not always easy to arrange to meet the individuals who had received audits or who had trained as Quality Checkers. Therefore for part of the responses in these stakeholder groups we have relied on opinions given to us from staff at the relevant organisations (this is highlighted in the list above). This is reflected in the financial value assigned – generally we could not agree a financial value for benefit described by a third party.

Many organisations and individuals fit into more than one category.

EXCLUDED

Independently of this evaluation, a number of people suggested that friends and family are an important stakeholder group. The theory goes that the friends and family would know whether people receiving services were happier, and would be able to talk about the difference that Quality Checker training had made to their friends.

This suggests three groups of family and friends:

1. Friends and family of people receiving the checks
2. Friends and family of people doing the checks (the Quality Checkers)
3. Friends and family of people who received Quality Checker training (whether they went on to become Quality Checkers or not)

I discussed this with the Quality Checkers and with staff directly involved with people who receive audits. The inclusion of these groups raises some important issues, and the general feeling was that an approach to friends and family would directly contradict the independent status of the people receiving support. This is covered in more detail in **Stakeholders identified but not included** on page 70.

1. Friends and family of people receiving checks
    a. Most people live full and active lives, and people receiving support to live independent lives may be involved in many projects, clubs, activities and schemes through the year and at any one time. People (like you or I) would not always discuss their activities with friends or family, when they see them at social occasions; and they might not be able to compare "before" and "after" – particularly this long after the audits took place
2. Friends and family of people doing the checks (the Quality Checkers)
    a. Are unlikely to discuss the minutiae of their jobs, or the questionnaires or surveys in a social context – in the same way that you and I don't discuss these with friends and family. In most cases Quality Checker friends and family would not know what a Quality Checker is. Two family members did agree to talk, and their comments are included in the section on Quality Checkers as a stakeholder
3. Friends and family of people receiving training

a. A combination of both of the above: friends and family want to talk about social activities and plan their joint activities, not question whether their independent friend is getting the support to be independent – that is the responsibility of the person.

Numbers of each stakeholder

We needed to get representative views from each stakeholder group, so we interviewed at least 3 in every group we talked to. This means that if we got different views, we could see if they broadly agreed or were totally different, a process known as triangulation.

We wanted to know both the corporate view, and what people thought individually.

How many did we interview in each group (we were able to ask about more than one type of stakeholder in some of the interviews)?

Stakeholder group	Interviews with management: Numbers of organisations	Interviews with people who were the direct recipients
People receiving support who had audits	4	5[4] (as a single group)
Quality Checker Trainees	5	6 (two groups of 3)
Organisations which provide health services	-	Not applicable
Organisations which provide social care services, including management	5	Not applicable
Staff at provider services	Not applicable	5
Similar organisations and competitors	2	-
Regulators, policy advisors, other advocacy groups	4	Not applicable
Commissioners of services	5	Not applicable

[4] I did not arrange many meetings with recipients of services because they will treat me as another "professional" and not necessarily give an unvarnished view, and because of the logistics (transport and support workers would be needed). After all, that's why the Quality Checkers are the best people to do User Experience audits. I managed a group interview with 5 people to check that they agreed with the benefits put forward by other groups on their behalf. They confirmed these views, which justifies the decision not to interview more.

How we asked for feedback

No paper questionnaires were used at all. They have a notoriously low response rate, especially amongst people with deprivation issues (Bradley and Stationery Office 2010, Lewis, Rosen et al. 2010). All of the interviews were semi-structured interviews, and were either by phone or face to face. Although the independent auditor is applying for an SROI accreditation, semi-structured interview is my preferred way of working; it is robust and reliable in experienced hands. I have extensive experience of using structured interview and focus groups, and during the course of the interview, was able to confirm that my choice of semi-structured interviews was able to generate the best and most consistent results.

Semi-structured interviews allow the interviewer to identify what the person with information knows, but don't know that they know, and coach them to reveal this information. It also allows the interviewer to quickly identify information that is required but the person doesn't know, and ask for an introduction to someone else who can provide this information. Structured interviews and surveys do not have this level of flexibility, and focus groups or open discussion often fails to address these important points (particularly as "numbers people" often don't feel comfortable in an unstructured environment).

How were the stakeholders involved?

Initially, Skills for People (both the service manager and the Quality Checkers) identified a number of customers of both audits and training, and other people they had contact with. Skills for People made the introduction by email.

The independent auditor then followed these introductions by email and telephone to ask permission to interview them.

In all cases, following an initial interview (usually by phone, sometimes in person) I wrote the notes from the interview and sent them to the person interviewed for verification, and any comments made (whether by phone or email) were immediately incorporated into the notes. During the interviews, I was advised to speak to some additional stakeholders, and followed up with interviews of these. We had identified the correct stakeholder groups first time around, as all additional stakeholders fitted into one of the existing stakeholder groups. Their input proved valuable for calculating financial equivalence, although many were not able to describe benefits they themselves had had as a result of the Quality Checker audits or training. The first interviews took place over a period from August to December 2010.

The notes from all of the interviews (including any corrections) were combined and the initial calculations of the value of each benefit (and averages between stakeholders) were then prepared as a collated Draft 1 document. I sent this to all interviewees involved for comment.

A second round of interviews took place during December 2010 to February 2011. This involved speaking to each interviewee both about the notes of their first interview, and the content of Draft 1 of the collated report (including comments on other people's responses). As a result of this second round of interviews, many people revised their estimates of benefit and understood how they too could assign values to their claimed benefits based on what other people had said/done. A combination of a general reduction of the first value placed on benefits, and putting a value on more of the previously unvalued benefits, resulted in approximately no change to the overall benefits claimed by stakeholders.

The second draft was sent out for comment, and comments incorporated to provide the basis for this document. The first and second drafts were designed to present information and not conclusions: this document is designed to be more accessible and to summarise the information.

Numbers of people in each stakeholder group involved in developing the theory of change for that group

Quality Checkers is a national service providing audits from Cornwall to London to the North West and North East of England, and Scotland. We wanted to clarify the Theory of Change, ie what the connection is between the Quality Checker audits and the benefits recorded in this report.

It was not possible to gather everyone (or even representative groups) into workshops to develop the theory of change collectively, so I recorded individual responses and then shared them with all of the stakeholders for comments, via the two draft documents highlighted above. This had an added advantage: according to the "Wisdom of Crowds"(Surowiecki 2005), the best combined result comes about when the people voicing opinions are independent and not influenced by each other. People may be influenced by the other people in a workshop; when each is interviewed independently then they will certainly speak their own mind uninfluenced.

Different stakeholders in the various stakeholder groups came up with the same benefits, the same connections between what the Quality Checkers did, and what benefits they identified. Most benefits were identified by 2 or more stakeholders (using different words but with the same content). The ones that were only identified by one stakeholder (Quality Checkers' value in the North East championing and coordinating voluntary organisations) had a relatively low or zero calculated financial value overall. The theory of change for each group and even each benefit has been corroborated by more than one individual stakeholder, and agreed and confirmed through the draft review process.

We identified around 29 benefits. If we count each time a stakeholder group identified a benefit, then there are 48 individual benefits and some can be grouped into a total of 29 benefit groups. Of these, we were able to estimate a financial value for 10. This doesn't mean that the other benefits aren't valuable – it only means that we couldn't agree on a value/ financial equivalence.

In **What Difference does it make – IMPACT**, I've included tables which show how each benefit is measured and calculated. I'd like to highlight that we have only included total values actually claimed by people who responded to the interviews – we haven't made any assumptions for other organisations. So if three respondents each claim £1000 for a benefit, then we record an average of £1000 per person, applied to 3 people = £3000 as the claimed value for that benefit. We have not applied benefits to other organisations which did not specifically identify that benefit during interviews.

What did we find? Outcomes and Evidence

The Impact Map illustrates the chain of causality, or costs invested/ incurred by each stakeholder group and what they got for it (the outputs, and outcomes). In this document I have presented notes to support the Impact Map.

The Quality Checkers make a large number of differences, but two are the most significant:

1. they inspired vulnerable people, adults with learning disabilities, to speak up for themselves, and to raise their expectations

2. they showed staff and supporting organisations that people with learning disabilities really do care about the environment they live in (even if they have significant communication difficulties), and that they want to live a full life, not just a safe one

let me explain in a little more detail.

Inputs, outputs and outcomes for each stakeholder group

In order to get something out, people have to put something in. The **inputs** may vary, from money (paid to Skills for People in order to purchase the Quality Checker audits or training), to time and effort.

The Quality Checkers typically get involved in workshops to get feedback, and produce a report. But this isn't the total of their **outputs.** People also took inspiration from the way the Quality Checkers work.

These outputs by themselves aren't the real benefit. The real benefit comes when something is done about the outputs. The **outcomes** are what happens, the benefits, and we have been able to put values against some of these.

The Inputs, Outputs and Outcomes are illustrated on the Impact map (separate enclosure).

Many of the outcomes (or benefits) could have a financial equivalent value applied. These fell broadly into two categories – those where the financial equivalent value is in fact real money saved, and where the financial equivalent is a "good" that people might be prepared to spend money on, but which doesn't actually represent money that can be saved directly. To give examples of both of these:

Real savings: if the provider of care services finds that staff sickness/absence improves, they save real money. They have to pay for the staff whether the staff are sick or working, and they have to pay for additional staff when staff are sick. So a decrease in sickness/ absence from 5.5% (industry standard and the level in the rest of the business) to 4.5% (the Real savings: if the provider of care services finds that staff sickness/absence improves, they save real money. They have to pay for the staff whether the staff are sick or working, and they have to pay for additional staff when staff are sick. So a decrease in sickness/ absence from 5.5% (industry standard and the level in the rest of the business) to 4.5% (the level of sickness/ absence in the part of the business where Quality Checker audits have taken place) means lower actual costs ie money that doesn't have to be spent providing this service.

Estimated value: for the people who receive audits – Inspiration from seeing "someone like them" in a professional role (ie the Expert by Experience Quality Checker. We've used academic research to make an estimate of the costs of medication and treatment for someone who is depressed, but the assumption that these costs will actually be saved is only an assumption.

Lastly, there are benefits or outcomes that I did not put a financial equivalence value on: examples include increased community involvement and turning out to vote.

Stakeholder Group	Inputs	Outputs	Outcomes = Benefits
People receiving support who had audits	• Time to take part in the audit • An organisation, either commission or provider, had to invest funds in buying the audits	• Conversations with a peer ("someone like them") who is a professional • 117 audits with organisations that I interviewed, taking place during the period of the scope of this study	• Inspiration that "somebody like them" is acting in a professional role

Table of Contents | The Social Return Co

Stakeholder Group	Inputs	Outputs	Outcomes = Benefits
			People who had audits did not typically pay for them themselves, and their input was not many cases the people with supported living were delighted to have company to talk to. Cost of audits is listed with the relevant stakeholder.
			Financial equivalence of "Inspiration" was calculated based on the costs of caring for per calculated the amount that depression is estimated to cost per depressed person and used only the figures for cost to NHS of medication and treatment (£462.86 in 2000). Since many people who receive support for independent living are on medication for depression, and according to the research, everyone who received audits would benefit in this area, we used Deadweight to assume 50% of people changed their medication/ treatment. Only 5 people were interviewed so the figure is calculated for these 5.

Other Outcomes which did not have a financial equivalence calculated were:

- Being listened to and having comments acted upon
- Community involvement
- Turning out to vote at the local and general elections
- Feedback from the Quality Checkers, and a form report
- Aspiration to take more control of their own life
- Initiatives such as better tenancy agreements, ho matching services and community involvement
- Opportunities such as selecting their own suppor worker

- Less frustrated so less challenging behaviour
- Initiatives such as more accessible tenancy agree & house matching

Negative Outcomes

I also asked what didn't happen because of the audits. This group were so happy to be listened to, and so happy that their requests were making a difference to where they lived, and they couldn't think of any negative consequences of the audits

Stakeholder Group	Inputs	Outputs	Outcomes = Benefits
Quality Checker Trainees	• Attending the training sessions • Payments made to people receiving support, and their support workers, to attend training sessions (transport, accommodation) • An organisation, either commission or provider, had to invest funds in purchasing the training	• In total, 201 people attended training courses, of whom we estimate 74 were self-advocates (the rest being support workers, managers etc). These reported the following benefits: • Being valued, being taught something new • Communication skills, skills that could get you a job • Network of new friends • An example: the Quality Checker trainers embodied strong values in a mixed team	• Learning new skills and an example of a new way of looking at the world; high aspirations • Paid work – sometimes a salary, sometimes running your own business

Stakeholder Group	Inputs	Outputs	Outcomes = Benefits

- More confidence (a new way of looking at the world) was estimated using preference me prefer, to be a Quality Checker or to go to Alton Towers?" and other preference values.

- The value of paid work to the Quality Checkers was simply calculated as the amount the wages were for Quality Checker work, and these costs are recognised in the costs to Commissioning organisations and providing organisations for purchasing audits. The remainder of the wages were from other sources unconnected with Quality Checkers.

Outcomes where I did not apply a Financial Equivalence include:

- Greater resilience to the knocks of life – the family member who spoke to me described before and after – when the Quality Checker received bad news she could isolate herself and contemplate (and attempt) suicide, whereas now that she has a purpose in life she can take bad news and process it, putting it into context with her activities and what she is still able to do

- Quality Checkers offer support for regional forums and practical advice and materials

I asked about negative outcomes.

The trainees didn't all go on to become Quality Checkers (fewer than half did), but they all came out of the courses more confident and more able to take the little knocks that life throws at you.

The only negative consequence anyone could tell me about was that some people aspired to paid work and yet weren't able to get a job, either because locally the Quality Checker team funding ran out, or because they never developed the confidence. On balance everyone felt that even this was better than not doing the training and not having a chance.

Stakeholder Group	Inputs	Outputs	Outcomes = Benefits
Organisations which provide social care services,	• Investment of money in purchasing audits • staff time being in attendance for the audits	• 220 audits completed by Worcester Supporting People team, who were trained as Quality Checkers by the QC team. A further 197 were performed by Quality Checkers team in Skills for People, Newcastle. • Organisations reported what they had changed	• An accurate picture of user experience which identified what needed to change, and in what ways • Reduction in cost of care • Increased actual business won • Reduced staffing costs

Stakeholder Group	Inputs	Outputs	Outcomes = Benefits

- Definite and real figures were available from the provider organisations to illustrate th because I have only used figures actually reported, the figures for Worcestershire Supporting People are additional and not duplicate to the figures for Advance UK or United Response

- Staff cost savings have been reported in two parts – reduced sickness/absence (a co disciplinary / turnover (a component in the overheads HR costs).

- following the audits, staff staff felt more involved with their clients and developed their l "support". This change in the relationship increased staff satisfaction, which was measured by the organisations as a reduction in staff sickness/absence from 5.5% to 4.5%.

- The audits identified inappropriate attitudes amongst senior staff which were bein attitudes, if left unidentified and unchecked, would have resulted in inappropriate behaviour (eg staff talking in front of clients in breach of confidentiality (because they didn't think the clients could understand); staff over-ruling client choice of house mates; staff allocating rooms in the clients' own homes as "staff rooms") which would have led to complaints and disciplinary investigation/ action. One organisation described in some detail the attitudes that the Quality Checkers identified in their report, staff retraining and the resulting reduced costs of disciplinary action and the expected disciplinary action from this situation if the Quality Checkers had not been involved. Other organisations confirmed this. In all of these organisations, they confirmed that they had expected a certain level of "staff going bad" and had not found other ways to reduce this.

Outcomes where I did not apply a Financial Equivalence include:

- Formal inclusion of User Experience in audits – this is a requirement for compliance v actually enforced so there is no actual financial penalty for failure

- Supporting people who are more confident that they will be listened to – this shows it behaviour. The costs are passed straight on to the commissioners of services

Stakeholder Group	Inputs	Outputs	Outcomes = Benefits
• Meeting charitable trust aims – this satisfies the charity trustees and donors, but concerned with the Quality Checkers, we concluded that charities would not be comfortable with any financial equivalence valuation • reporting national benchmarks (REACH standards)– this is expected to reduce tl can refer to national standards and national monitoring methodology, rather than spelling out the local requirements in great detail. It is also likely to reduce the cost of failed contracts and litigation. In both cases, the costs are borne by the commissioner rather than the provider of a service **Negative Outcomes:** One organisation did report that since they had increased confidence, users spoke up a lot more about the things they wanted. This was reflected in the number of minor complaints recorded – the number of minor complaints per year rocketed from 60 to 77. But these were easy to sort out and meant that far fewer complaints were left to become more serious.			

Stakeholder Group	Inputs	Outputs	Outcomes = Benefits
Similar organisations and competitors	• purchasing training and supporting people to attend training • Cost of support given to allow people more flexibility, eg production of accessible information and staffing to explain it • Access to Quality Checkers/ Skills for People for ideas and new service development	• Teams trained to provide Quality Checker audits • Supported choices eg production of accessible, Tenancy agreements, House matching services	• Reducing the numbers of serious misunderstandings within shared houses, which result in the need for emergency moves and emergency accommodation • More vulnerable people into employment and independent living making their own choices of house mates and community involvement

Stakeholder Group	Inputs	Outputs	Outcomes = Benefits
• Some of the advocacy organisations similar to Skills for People asked for their own Checkers. Others offer very different services, and said that the Quality Checker reports that they saw inspired them to do new and innovative things such as the Accessible Tenancy Agreement and House Matching (some have extended this to Friend Matching and so on)			
• In most cases, the financial equivalence value assigned is an actual amount of mor This is the amount of money that doesn't need to be spent because the user experience of their clients is better following the Quality Checker audits. The reader should note that these organisations spend considerable resources (usually provided by the Local Authority) improving the life opportunities and experience of people better, and the full cost of the work they do has been included in the costs, although only the improvement attributable to Quality Checker audits has been included in the Outcomes			
• These organisations are dedicated to improving life experience, therefore it is likely ways to improve the lives of those they support. They themselves gave high levels of attribution to the Quality Checkers, but in the light of their dedication, I have assigned 50% likelihood that they would have come up with something similar (or achieved 50% of the result) as Deadweight, and assigned a further 50% that they may have been developing something that was no longer needed (Displacement)			
Outcomes not given a financial equivalence value:			
• Measuring user experience using national standards – although this was considere interviewed, we agreed that the principal beneficiaries are the commissioners of services who actually pay for the services offered, and therefore we've assigned a single value for this benefit, which is in the section on the stakeholder "Commissioners"			

Stakeholder Group	Inputs	Outputs	Outcomes = Benefits
Regulators, policy advisors, other advocacy groups	• Time in conversation with Quality Checkers and Skills for People	• 23 organisations spoken to who discussed benefits • Access to reports on provider services (with permission of the provider) which gives both qualitative and quantitative evidence to support policy change • Evidence that user experience audits will highlight different requirements to previous inspection reports	• Confidence that the national agenda "Valuing People" is being met • Avoiding costs for inspections and avoiding substantial costs if a public enquiry resulted from an error

Stakeholder Group	Inputs	Outputs	Outcomes = Benefits

- The regulator has a statutory duty to ensure that user experience is taken into accoun who receive support: "no decision about me, without me". The regulator has been able to use the Quality Checker audits as evidence for this, and the regulator (Department of Health) cited saving £5000 per organisation per year in pure regulatory activity

- An independent consultant described the public enquiry in Cornwall. This was outside no total costs have been reported, but the Quality Checker audits would have prevented this. The consensus is that Quality Checker audits quickly identify attitudes and behaviours likely to cause problems in the future, so a situation such as happened in this case simply doesn't arise, with audits at regular intervals (the situation in Cornwall may have been developing over 15 years or more). The Cornwall public enquiry may have cost over £10.5million. However the cost would be borne by the Commissioners (next stakeholder group – below)

I asked about negative consequences

The people I spoke to were full of respect for the work of the Quality Checkers, and the inspiration they gave to so many adults with learning disabilities. Naturally the methods might change, and naturally it is heavily dependent on the individuals who lead each team, but it was highly successful.

The most frequently highlighted complaint was that different local authorities and different care providers were trying to develop their own ways of measuring user experience, probably (in one person's cynical view) to avoid being benchmarked against other organisations. It's the same process as happens with SROI – the moment you have a popular benchmark then people look for excuses to avoid being measured.

- None of this would have happened without Quality Checkers, and the regulators belie' Checkers is sufficient to overcome this problem with time.

Stakeholder Group	Inputs	Outputs	Outcomes = Benefits
Commissioners of services	• Investing money in purchasing audits (see above)	• Audits performed (117 with interviewed organisations in the period of this report) • Feedback and formal reports highlighting specific changes providers need to make, and best practice that can be shared • Evaluation against nationally agreed criteria (REACH standards) using a national standard methodology	• Looking after the needs and wants of their constituency (adults with learning disabilities) • this also reduces the direct cost of "frustrated" and "challenging" behaviour, which commissioners pay for • Provider organisations become more innovative, and more open to new ways of doing things • Reduced numbers of cases of contractual non-compliance which reduces cost of litigation • Avoiding an expensive mistake (eg Cornwall)

Stakeholder Group	Inputs	Outputs	Outcomes = Benefits
• This group are probably the biggest single beneficiary of the Quality Checker audits performing the audits (which the commissioners often pay for). They are required to improve the life experience for people receiving support			
• Costs of supporting adults with learning disabilities vary greatly depending on the le support. The commissioner pays the care provider for this service, but if a client moves from basic support to moderate or high level support needs, then the commissioner has to find the money to pay the care provider, which can amount to a considerable change (Average cost/year to provide support at basic level was £4,166, compared with extra support for frustrated behaviour at £15,479 and where a person exhibits "challenging" behaviour the costs varied between £75,000 and £175,000 per year (averaged at £133,333). The Quality Checker audits were reported to reduce levels of frustrated and challenging behaviours considerably. Because of the small numbers of people exhibiting "challenging" behaviours, for this study I decided to exclude "Challenging" behaviour costs and only include the verifiable decrease in costs for caring for those people who no longer needed extra support because of "frustrated" behaviours.			
• Expectations about the support people should receive have changed – the commis: to be innovative and responsive. Unfortunately many still aren't and the Quality Checker audits often act as a wake-up call, encouraging the care providers to be more innovative and flexible			
• The use of the Quality Checker audits also has a direct impact on contractual non-c (the REACH standards) means that care providers know what is expected of them (and have the same standards nation-wide which makes it easier to change business processes to comply, and to report compliance). So the costs of preparing contracts is lower, and the cost of litigation is lower			

Description of indicators and data sources for each stakeholder group

Of course it's important to understand how we measured, and what we measured.

In most cases, they were able to go back to their files and find out the information I needed to know, statistics over time, costs, and so on. In some cases, I could only use what they could remember.

The independent auditor spoke to each of the stakeholders who had agreed to be interviewed.

Stakeholder Group	Benefit	Indicators	Data Source
People receiving support who had audits	• Inspiration that "somebody like them" is acting in a professional role • Being listened to • Community involvement • Being able to contribute to their community • Taking control • Less "frustrated" behaviour	• I talked to people who received the audits, and their advocates (support workers, team leaders, managers in organisations which provided care who knew most about the clients) and identified suitable indicators such as • Numbers of people who could remember "someone like them i professional role" • Numbers involved in the community or turning out to vote • Numbers selecting their own support worker. • The indicators and data source for this group are listed in the Impact Map	

Stakeholder Group	Benefit	Indicators	Data Source
Quality Checker Trainees	• Learning new skills and an example of a new way of looking at the world; high aspirations • Paid work – sometimes a salary, sometimes running your own business	• Numbers of people who reported increased confidence, or whose support workers reported increased confidence • People in employment – Quality Checkers • People in employment as Quality Checkers and other employment • Amount being paid to people in employment	• Conversations with two groups of people who had received training and become Quality Checkers • Conversations with organisations that have developed teams of Quality Checkers • Organisation records of who is in what employment

Stakeholder Group	Benefit	Indicators	Data Source
Organisations which provide social care services, including management experiences	• An accurate picture of user experience which identified what needed to change, and in what ways • Reduction in cost of care • Increased actual business won • Reduced staffing costs	• Reduction in total costs of providing care • Actual additional business won • Reduced levels of sickness/absence from staff HR records, and the financial value in this (as other staff have to be paid to cover absences) • Numbers of (and severity of) disciplinary actions, and the cost of these	• Costs of providing care, numbers of installations and staff costs from provider organisation records • documented information on costs, and incidence e.g. (Kegan 1978, Heywood 2001, Findlay and Cartwright 2002, Findlay 2003, Fyson, Tarleton et al. 2007, Hirsch 2008, DH 2009, Worcs Reach Review Team 2009, Kilsby and Beyer 2010, Worcs SP team 2010, Zappalà and Lyons 2010)
Similar organisations and competitors	• Reducing the numbers of serious misunderstandings within shared houses, which result in the need for emergency moves and emergency accommodation • More vulnerable people into employment and independent living making their own choices of house mates and community involvement	• Numbers of house crises caused by misunderstandings, which are avoided when tenants choose their own house mates • Numbers of new services/ accessible documents prepared each year	• Conversations with individuals representing similar organisations as part of stakeholder interviews • Numbers of crises requiring emergency accommodation from housing support organisations supporting this client group

Stakeholder Group	Benefit	Indicators	Data Source
Regulators, policy advisors, other advocacy groups	• Confidence that the national agenda "Valuing People" is being met • Avoiding costs for inspections and avoiding substantial costs if a public enquiry resulted from an error	• numbers of organisations audited successfully by Quality Checkers which means the number of organisations that the regulator does not need to audit itself (user experience audits)	• Conversations with the relevant individuals • Desk-based research e.g. (Heywood 2001, Snell 2007, Hirsch 2008, Lovell 2008, Michael 2008, DH 2009, DH 2009)
Commissioners of services	• Looking after the needs and wants of their constituency (adults with learning disabilities) • this also reduces the direct cost of "frustrated" and "challenging" behaviour, which commissioners pay for • Provider organisations become more innovative, and more open to new ways of doing things • Reduced numbers of cases of contractual non-compliance which reduces cost of litigation • Avoiding an expensive mistake (eg Cornwall)	• Care provider organisations which are more responsive to change • Numbers of cases of litigation for contractual non-compliance • Numbers of adults receiving support who exhibit "frustrated" or "challenging" behaviour, and the costs/ cost savings of this	• Conversations with relevant individuals representing Commissioner organisations (Learning Disabilities Partnership Boards) • Figures for the relevant metrics • Existing cost/benefits evaluations e.g. (Stein 2006, Worcs Reach Review Team 2009, Worcs SP team 2010)

Quantity of inputs, outputs and outcomes for each stakeholder group

One of the biggest challenges was to get numbers from what is essentially a "number phobic" group.

Typically people who go into health and social care take this vocation because they enjoy working with people. Many find it very difficult to step away from the uniqueness of each individual, and count the number of people they have seen with a particular severity of the condition, or a particular support package need. This of course makes it very difficult to plan ahead, and that is exactly what we are trying to achieve with this report. In many cases, I had to speak to a different people from each organisation in order to understand what changes, by how much, and what impact it has; and also to understand how much could be attributed to the Quality Checker audits, and how much would have happened anyway.

As I highlighted earlier, although the stakeholder groups between them identified around 48 benefits, these broadly fall into 29 benefit groups. In order to avoid double counting, each benefit is described in the context of the stakeholder group, but the value of the whole benefit group is calculated within only one stakeholder group, and the whole value assigned to that stakeholder group. This avoids long debates on how much should be apportioned to each stakeholder group, when we know the total will add up to the same number. Of course different groups may have different benefits, but the above was a robust approach.

Some notes on length of time, financial proxies, deadweight, attribution, drop-off, and displacement.

A large number of benefits are described in the Impact Map; I have also listed some benefits which could only be described in qualitative terms because of their nature, because of disagreement in the published literature about how to assign a value, or because the stakeholders (interviewees) and myself decided it would be inappropriate to assign a financial value.

I've tried to describe within each benefit where the figures come from, how we have agreed financial equivalent values, sources of the information, and the different stakeholder groups which claim the same benefit (and where the financial equivalent value has been recorded).

Deadweight – what would have happened anyway

The semi-structured interviews discussed the deadweight and therefore focussed on what was different because of Quality Checkers, as opposed to everything that had changed and then subtracting deadweight afterwards. The Quality Checkers are virtually unique (the other peer review teams around the country who work with adults with learning disabilities are teams that were trained by the Quality Checkers from Skills for People), and care provider organisations and commissioners said that they used to expect a level of failure and had not managed to date to identify either a way to improve the situation, or even the possibility that it might work! The claim for most benefits is that there was no "it would have improved anyway", nor were people or organisations engaged in programmes or policies to improve the situation on anything like the scale of the Quality Checkers (Displacement). In a few cases organisations were making changes, and we had to make estimates, and here we have compared and triangulated between a number of interviewees.

In at least one case, though, an organisation had just appointed a new manager who initiated a whole range of changes at the same time, one of which was Quality Checker audits. Because the manager was new we had trouble allocating Deadweight.

Displacement – when good outcomes for one stakeholder become bad outcomes for another

I took care to ask at each interview "what wasn't good about the Quality Checker audits?". Everyone I spoke to was delighted – there were no negative outcomes and even the unexpected consequences turned out to be positive.

There were a couple of comments made which resulted in good results for some people and less good results for others, though as these were generally in the same stakeholder group they probably don't count as Displacement. For example some Quality Checker trainees got all fired up and then couldn't get jobs, whereas others got jobs because they were fired up.

On reviewing the interview notes I asked the question "could all the focus on the organisations that have audits, take attention away from those that don't? Or could the people that have audits themselves, end up with better support than the ones that don't?".

The answer appears to be "No". Quality Checker audits change attitudes, so members of staff read an audit about one person receiving support, and change their attitudes to everyone they support. And the savings in resources needed because of the Quality Checker reports often free up resources to target poorly performing care providers. Perhaps the most obvious example of this is one of the benefits that Commissioners reported – that when some care providers had Quality Checker audits, a great many care providers responded by being more flexible and open to more innovation.

Attribution – how much was due to other initiatives

In every case, the stakeholders estimated how much of the benefit they attributed to the Quality Checkers. The Quality Checkers produce reports, and organisations and individuals have to act on them. In some cases, for example changes in attitude, the Quality Checkers have had most of the benefit is attributed to them, because the change in attitude does not require much effort on the part of the individual – it happens unconsciously if the report is sufficiently moving. In other cases, where the Quality Checkers made recommendations and the provider organisation acted upon them (for example, to an organisation that was under scrutiny for failing services, and then turned the service around), then we attributed a greater part of the change to the organisation's efforts, even though it was the Quality Checker audit initiated the change.

Duration and Drop-off - how long the change will last, and how much change will be left after a year.

The change brought about by the Quality Checkers is not like a direct intervention, for example putting someone into work, or funding a support worker. The biggest impact of the Quality Checkers was that they change attitudes. This showed when I interviewed the Quality Checkers themselves. I asked what would happen if the service received no more funding; they answered that they would start by feeling vulnerable and going back to being frightened, but within a month or two they would remember that they had been strong before, and they would begin to stand up for themselves. The change would last a lifetime.

Of course, there are some situations where the benefits would not last so long. I discussed with the interviewees what percentage drop-off figure (or fraction drop-off figure, if that was the way they thought) would be appropriate. The drop-off describes how much of the change will still happen a year after the Quality Checkers had done whatever they do, and then two years after. A 25% (or ¼) drop-off means that only 75% (or ¾) of the benefit continues in year 2, and 56% (75%*75% or 9/16) continues in year 3.

Even this can be complicated: the Quality Checkers inspire people to stand up for themselves, and the effect is actually cumulative. As more people see these inspired people, they too would become inspired. This would normally give a negative drop-off, which I haven't used in the calculations.

So throughout the descriptions of the benefits, I've included the descriptions of sources, financial proxies, attributions, drop-offs, and percentages applicable.

What Difference does it make – IMPACT

The impacts are explained on the Impact Map (paired with this document). In this section of the SROI report I will summarise the results from the Impact Map and discuss some of the key outcomes and their importance, and the assumptions and sensitivity

People receiving support who had audits

The people who received audits are adults with learning disabilities, who want to live independently (in their own home or shared accommodation) and who receive support usually in the form of a personal assistant, to help them.

> "What would you want in YOUR home?"
>
> Mike Maguire – Worcestershire supporting people services

The support they receive has to meet certain functional standards, such as being compliant with health and safety, and the people have to be involved in their own development plan. What has proved much more difficult is to discover on a consistent basis whether the person enjoys her life, and is actually enjoying the same choices that other people do.

It was with this in mind that the quality checkers were set up. Many adults with learning disabilities who receive support feel vulnerable, and do not feel comfortable criticising the people who support them, even when they are dissatisfied with their support. By talking to someone like themselves, an expert by experience, they reveal what they really think.

Perhaps most important impact that the quality checkers contribute is the example of themselves: many people receiving support feel as though they are incapable of doing anything useful, and have resigned themselves to needing support all of their lives. In some cases, they feel that no one is listening to them, and they resort to frustrated or challenging behaviours to get attention. But the quality checkers are "people like them", who are performing a professional role using their unique skills!

> "People think staff do not listen to them when they complain"
>
> Dawn McGreevy – South Tyneside Direct Services

Everybody said how important this was to them, and their support staff were amazed that they had remembered so long after the audit itself. I was looking for financial equivalence figure that would be relevant for people taking more interest in their own lives, and I use the value given for depression. I use the direct treatment cost, which is approximately 1/30th of the total cost of depression per person(Emler 2001, Thomas and Morris 2003, Alleyne 2009). That gives an impact for the five people I interviewed of £1089 (taking into account deadweight – what would have happened anyway, displacement, attribution). Over five years (including drop-off and duration), this means the total impact of £1429 (see impact map).

People receiving support, and the people who supported them, described a large number of other impacts that had been brought about because of the quality checkers, examples such as:

- being listened to and having their comments acted upon (and feeling empowered)

- attending community events instead of those designed for adults with learning disabilities

- making a contribution to their community by attending political hustings in turning out to vote

- various opportunities to take control of their own lives, including selecting their own support worker

- and less frustrated or challenging behaviour

Although some of these can be valued, I have avoided double counting by assigning the value to the stakeholder to whom it is most relevant – for example, less frustrated or challenging behaviour is most relevant to the commissioners of services who have to pay for different levels of support (different numbers of hours).

Overall, this stakeholder group did not believe that it cost anything to be involved in quality checker audits, and we were able to assign a financial equivalence value to them (Total Present Value PV based on 3.5% inflation) of £1368 over five years.

Generally, care is improving for adults with learning disabilities, therefore we are signed a 50% deadweight value. However, the stakeholders and their support to criticise that they did not have other programs in place (displacement 0%), and that it was the actual presence of the quality checkers themselves (experts by experience) that made the difference (attribution 0%).

Quality Checker Trainees

Quality Checker trainees are the people who received training from Skills for People Quality Checkers Team. The training includes communication skills; understanding the REACH standards (which helps people to understand standards and quality, and confidentiality); the Quality Checker audit method (how to interview, what to do to get a person to talk or to communicate in whatever means they can, planning an interview and carrying it out); reporting and putting the responses in context; a whole lot of skills which are relevant to many other jobs.

I interviewed two different groups of Quality Checkers, three in each group, and their answers were broadly similar. In order to triangulate properly, I would be looking for two out of three who broadly agree(Surowiecki 2005). I have two out of two who broadly agree so this satisfies the criterion. I also spoke to a number of advocates relaying feedback from their own groups of Quality Checkers, who were also consistent in their answers.

Quality checkers described how the training equipped them to take a greater part in their communities, to build networks and friends, and to get jobs[5]. Universally there was high praise for the training, how much they enjoyed it, and how much more confident they felt. The training courses obviously have a cost (the cost to the organisations that pay for the training courses, plus the cost to the organisations who support people to attend those training courses) but this stakeholder group did not pay anything themselves. We have assigned the cost of the number of hours they attended the benefits they receive pro rata(Emerson, Hatton et al. 2011), in order to estimate costs to the stakeholder group.

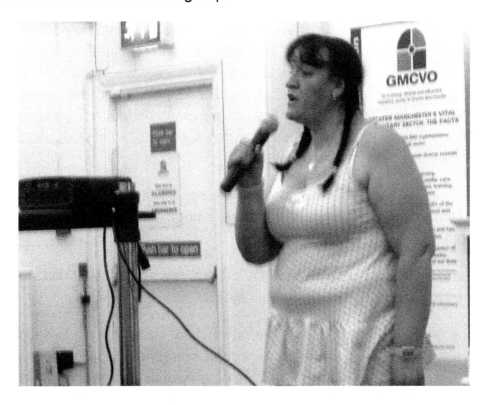

Overall, these stakeholders invested £1,527 (74 trainees attended courses in the period in scope, at approximately 12 hours training and receiving Disability Living

---

[5] Skills for People recorded the numbers attending courses, but made no distinction whether they were self-advocates, support workers, staff at commissioners etc. A small number of organisations were able to say how many people on the course they had purchased, were self-advocates, and how many were in employment, and what kind of employment. These averages were used to extrapolate.

Allowance averaging £64.34 per week – total benefits were not used in this calculation only the proportion attributable to adults with learning disabilities)(Emerson, Hatton et al. 2011).

The value these stakeholders gained from the joy and sense of purpose(DH 2009) of being a Quality Checker was determined using Preference Methods – I asked them in a group environment what they would prefer – to be a Quality Checker or to have various things of known value (tea and a cake in a nearby café, day trip to Alton Towers, holiday to Disneyland Florida – all things that they had done and understood).

The amount the received from paid work was simply determined by asking the Quality Checkers and their support staff how much Quality Checkers actually earned, on average, taking into account the ones who were trained but weren't actually working (and therefore earned nothing). These figures are much lower than the calculated wages in (Kilsby and Beyer 2010), but Kilsby's figures were based on working time of 15-16 hours per week. The Quality Checker trainees I spoke to, and the ones supported by organisations I spoke to, would not be able to work more than 3-4 hours per week because of their physical health.

We also estimated the value that the training gave because it made people more resilient to the ups and downs of life. This was based on the interviews with family members; one said that her sister would brood for days or weeks over the slightest bit of bad news before she became a Quality Checker, but when she received the news that she had breast cancer, her first action was to go into work and immerse herself with her friends and colleagues. As the sister said, "without Quality Checkers she wouldn't still be here".

I based my financial equivalence value on the amount that people would be prepared to pay for a higher quality environment to have a happier life experience, given their limited resources and limited ability to pay.

 Over 5 years, taking into account all of the factors, the total amount this stakeholder group gained can be read from the Impact Map at NPV of £135,694.

Although many quality checker teams are now active, and some organisations have developed similar services for vulnerable groups, or services which recognise the new-found awareness (!) that adults with learning disabilities are people like you and I, everybody I spoke to said that this came out of the quality checker initiative. Therefore we agreed that deadweight should be 0% – these benefits would not have been achieved without them.

In many cases, the levels of depression and frustration, and progress moving people into jobs would have caused some other activities, though this had not been considered a priority (displacement, generally low percentage). As we noted above, there are now other initiatives, inspired by the quality checkers, therefore the attribution to the quality checker audits varies between 100% (0% attribution to other causes) and 50% (other causes represent 50% of the benefit).

The rate of drop-off has been determined on a benefit by benefit basis, as has the duration.

Organisations which provide social care services

I interviewed a number of organisations which provide care services, including services owned by the local authority, and services provided by charities. Broadly, their responses were similar.

The organisations which provide support (care providers) were one of the two main stakeholder groups who invested in audits and training, the other being the commissioners of services (the people who pay). Across the organisations interviewed, they purchased 197 audits plus the 220 audits performed by Worcestershire Supporting People quality checkers team, and spent £17,120 on audits, £19,165 on staff to support the audits, and £21,934 on training.

The key benefits that they gained in return were

- accurate information on the user experience (which enabled them to make the right changes to improve care), for which one organisation had prepared a detailed report on the costs of care without the audits and following the audits(Worcs Reach Review Team 2009, Worcs SP team 2010)

> *"Trustees report that they now get the same message from board members as they do when they visit people receiving support. Commissioners report that they have much more confidence in this organisation, and preferentially award more contracts to provide support, because it is clear that the quality of the service is very high"*
>
> Dave Young –Advance UK

- increased business in the form of additional contracts to provide support to adults with learning disabilities, through the changes they had implemented as a result of the audits

- reduction in staff costs through sickness/absence reduction from 5.5% staff days to 4.5%

- reduction in management costs through a reduction in staff turnover and reduction in the time and activity needed for disciplinary costs

> *"In one shared house, the support workers and management put a FIRE EXIT sign on one of the doors, to meet a health and safety requirement. People sharing the house pointed out that the support workers themselves would never have a FIRE EXIT sign in their living room.*
>
> *How many more times do we forget that we're working with real people?"*
>
> Dave Young – Advance UK

These benefits can be examined in the Impact Map. In total, NPV terms, they were cumulatively worth £957,813 over 5 years.

Similar organisations and competitors

The interviews covered a number of advocacy groups who work specifically with adults with learning disabilities. These organisations do different things to provide support, such as helping people into independent supported living, or house matching, or helping them get more involvement in the local community and to have fuller social lives.

These organisations spent £89,629 on training and supporting people to attend training, and a further £91,644 on staffing costs and resources to provide the accessible services (eg a team to advise people on their options when they want to move home or choose to share with a friend).

The organisations told me that he involvement of Quality Checkers reduced the number of break-ups in shared housing because people chose who they shared with on the basis of friendship and compatibility rather than because someone needed to be housed. They also supported people to move, supported people to become more independent, supported more people into employment(DH 2009) and were able with the help of Quality Checkers to develop more services. The total return they were able to attribute to Quality Checker audits, taking into account all of the factors and valued at present day figures (NPV) was £47,160.

> *"Quality Checkers are very focussed on taking action. Skills for People started with the idea of getting the user experience, and from this idea developed the REACH standards. This was followed by a training pack that we could pilot, followed by a training course that meant many organisations were able to do their own audits of user experience. This benefited self-advocates receiving support, and it provided valuable employment and pride for the newly trained Quality Checkers. Now QC are changing a whole culture so that involving people, really involving them, is becoming normal"*
>
> Steve Thompson – Sunderland People First

Regulators, policy advisors, other advocacy groups

The Department of Health, together with independent consultants and regional organisations want to make sure the Valuing People Now agenda carries on, and other advocacy groups are also interested in what the Quality Checkers do.

I spoke to a number of stakeholders in this group, including Department of Health (Valuing People lead) (DH) and Care Quality Commission (Adults with learning disabilities lead) (CQC). They don't actually invest anything themselves with the Quality Checkers, since they don't either purchase audits or training. But they are a very interested observer.

"Quality Checkers were brought in post-Cornwall, after the scandal in Budock Hospital (caring for people with learning disabilities). People who received support, support staff, and management were frightened and secretive, and didn't speak their minds at meetings. People with learning disabilities were told they had to take on a lot of new roles, and they were scared.

The Quality Checkers course was a defining point for many people, helping them realise that they had rights and responsibilities.

People stood up at the Partnership Board to demand jobs."

Sam Sly, health and social care consultant – Enough is Enough
and external Change Team for Cornwall Partnership Trust

The statutory priority for DH and CQC is to ensure that people's views are heard, "no decision about me without me". Other advocacy groups have the same priority - they don't have a statutory responsibility. The Quality Checker audits, by experts by experience and entirely focussed on ensuring the user voice is heard, fulfil this aim.

So I asked how this could be valued. Both DH and CQC are required to audit organisations to ensure they are compliant with the law and meet the standards for delivering care. CQC will have to audit the organisations anyway, regardless of the Quality Checker audits, whereas DH proposed that it would cost £5000 per organisation, specifically for the Valuing People audits regardless of other audits required. DH has accepted audits on 23 organisations, and with an allowance for displacement, attribution, and drop-off, this has an NPV over five years of £41,512.

Deadweight was taken as 0%, because the alternative to the quality checker audits were the audits the DH itself would have to perform (£5000). We use displacement (50%) to reference other possible schemes which might be acceptable to DH, and an attribution of 50% for the input the organisations themselves provide. Since organisations would need to be reordered did for valuing people every 2 to 3 years, we use a duration of three years, and drop-off of 67% per year.

The regulators also felt it important to highlight the value of the use of national standards. National standards, and the National method of measuring compliance with those standards makes it much easier for Providers (who are often national in their scope) to deliver care that takes into account user experience; they can deliver particular standards throughout their organisation, rather than having different standards to deliver in different parts of the country. It also makes it much easier to specify in the contract compliance is required, and reduces the likelihood of litigation between Commissioner and care provider, because there is a clear understanding of what the standards mean. These costs are referred to within the section on the stakeholder group of commissioners.

An independent consultant pointed out that if mistakes are made (due to lack of user involvement, or failure to take into account for staff attitudes) then expensive public enquiries can result. A recent example was the problems emerging during "campus re-provisioning" in Cornwall; although this public enquiry was very expensive in terms of legal fees, and probably even more expensive in terms of the actions that local authorities had to take to rectify the situation, it occurred before April 2008, in other words, before the start of the scope of this analysis. With the quality checkers are avoided the need for public enquiry? Many party said this is exactly what they would have done, so we have assigned a deadweight of 25%. Would anything else of come up to ensure that the clients receive the care they deserved? Well there were few problems with campus reprovisioning in other parts of England, so we have assigned 25% displacement value. Then we have used the attribution value to recognise that this public enquiry occurred outside of the dates of the scope, by assigning 100% attribution to other causes.

Commissioners of services

Commissioners of services (usually the local authority social services department) are the statutory bodies responsible for ensuring that adults with learning disabilities receive appropriate support, care and attention. They are the people who have the most interest in getting good services, and the most ability to make sure that this happens.

Commissioners establish contracts with providers of care services, and in the they usually contracts specify what levels of service they expect: for example, the provider has to make sure that the support it gives is safe, and keeps both staff and people who receive services safe. With the Quality Checker audits, commissioners can now add user experience into the contract, and say that the provider has to make sure that the user has a good experience.

Commissioning organisations probably have the most to gain from these audits, for the simple reason that one of the most expensive components of providing support for adults with learning disabilities is the number of hours per week support that people need.

At a basic level of support, people require between two and seven hours of support per week. Averaged over a number of different organisations, this amounted to £4166 per year. People with much more severe disabilities may require much more support, but this will not be affected by the quality checker audits, therefore we have concentrated on the development of "frustrated" or "challenging" behaviour.

Frustrated or challenging behaviour are very likely to occur where someone feels that they have no say – they are not being listened to. Someone can become unpredictable and throw things, which requires extra support – on average 14 hours per week extra support. The cost per year of supporting someone exhibiting frustrated behaviour averaged around £15,479.

Where someone feels completely powerless, that when they try to communicate, they are ignored, they may become violent – referred to as "challenging behaviour". The support costs escalate rapidly, since 24-hour cover is needed, and staff cannot be left on their own. Even in a shared living environment, the cost per person varies from £75,000-£175,000 per year, averaging at £133,333.

Commissioners and organisations providing care services observed that the mere fact of the quality checkers audit made a substantial difference to the numbers of people who felt they were not being listened to and started to exhibit these behaviours, probably because they felt inspired to see "people like them" in professional roles and been listened to. The audits themselves confirmed that the client had been listened to, since they could remember what they had asked to be changed, and could see it being changed. The reduction in numbers of people exhibiting "frustrated" behaviour was relatively easy to quantify, from 115 (across for organisations – 6.9%), to 52 (post audits – 2.1%). The numbers of people exhibiting "challenging" behaviour was more difficult to justify, since numbers of people exhibiting challenging behaviour are generally very small, and it would be difficult to prove statistically that the change was a real change, or natural variation. Therefore we have only used a financial value based on the change in the numbers of people showing "frustrated" behaviours.

In this case, both Commissioner organisations and provider organisations admitted that they expected a certain level of frustrated behaviour, and the 6.9% recorded was what they had come to expect. Therefore they did not have any special measures to try to reduce this further, since they thought this was the natural level of frustrated behaviour. This gave us a deadweight figure of 10% (natural decline over time in the levels of frustration), but displacement of 0% (no other activities planned), and an attribution of 0% (no other activities in place to try to reduce frustrated behaviour).

Commissioners also recorded that organisations who provide care were more responsive after they had seen quality checker audits than before, and more inclined to be innovative. They applied a financial value to this by estimating the legal and administrative costs of moving a contract from one provider to another, which they had had to do in previous years. They then made an estimate of the number of organisations which were now more responsive, and use this as the basis of this calculation.

As a separate calculation, commissioners identified the cost of individual "non-compliance" cases, where a single instance of care required either management intervention, or litigation. They were able to give costs across all severities of non-compliance, and estimate from this the average cost.

For both a reduction in the number of contracts that need to be moved, and a reduction in the times they had to take action to avoid non-compliance for a single person, we gave a deadweight of 10% (we would expect this to naturally improve), and a displacement of 10% (some initiatives would be put into place, although the levels of non-compliance or contract movement were considered "normal" which would reduce the likelihood of bringing in new initiatives to improve this situation).

Taking all of these factors into account, the NPV Return over five years for commissioners was around £1,745,476.

Analysis of the investment required

Of course, there has been quite a lot of investment in Quality Checkers and audits. The Quality Checkers themselves were set up with a grant from the North Tyneside Learning Disabilities Partnership Board.

The Quality Checkers make an on-going income by charging for audits and training. The audits typically take much longer than a professional auditor might take – interviewees are given plenty of time to say what they need to say, whereas a professional auditor will typically visit a whole organisation of a maximum of two hours, and collect all the information during that time. The Quality Checkers were able to provide me with information on the amount of income they had had from each organisation for their services (shown on the pie chart below as "QC Audits" and "QC Training").

Organisations which decided to train their own Quality Checkers were also able to account for the amount they had invested in travel, meetings, support etc for their own Quality Checkers during training courses (shown on the chart below as "Support time" and "Staff time".

Organisations that had teams of Quality Checkers (trained by the original team) also used them for audits, and the cost of these audits are listed as "Own Audits". Note that this is broadly equivalent to the amount that the Quality Checkers received in wages.

Lastly (on the pie chart, at least), people invested their own time in attending the training courses and other meetings, without getting paid for it. This is shown as "Own Time".

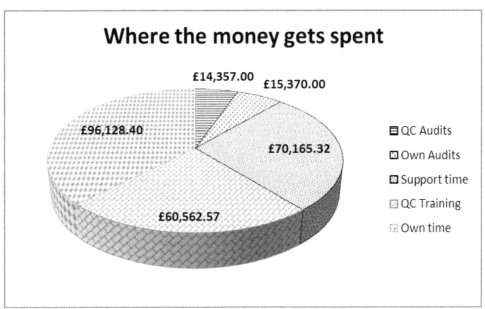

Where the money gets spent

£14,357.00 £15,370.00

£96,128.40

£70,165.32

£60,562.57

- QC Audits
- Own Audits
- Support time
- QC Training
- Own time

Total expenditure during the scope period was £256,583.

The total impact

For reasons described above, many of the benefits either had a financial value calculated (representing money that was no longer needed to provide care, even though the care had improved in quality; this money could be spent on other things e.g. other services), or had a financial equivalence estimated in consultation with stakeholders (this money cannot typically be taken and spent on other things, since it represents preferences, attitudes etc). One or two did not have financial equivalence values assigned, for reasons that the stakeholders felt strongly that it would be inappropriate to do so.

All benefits (social return) were calculated over a five-year period projected into the future, using a discount rate of 3.5% (government standard(Treasury 2003)), and using the values for duration (number of years where any benefit is observed) and drop-off (the amount of benefit the remaining for each year after the first year).

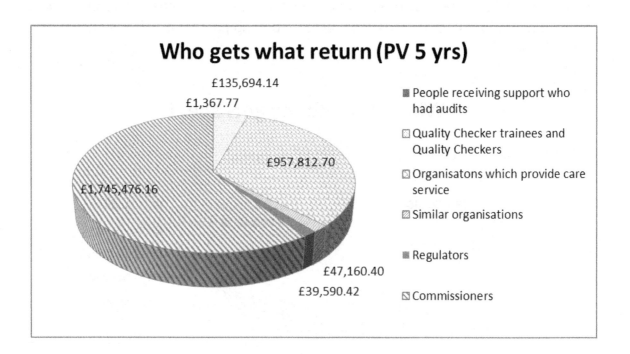

Overall Total present value (PV) over five years is £2,670,518. The major beneficiaries are the commissioners (who spent £3,874 million on Adults <65 with learning disabilities in England(Communities & Local Government 2011, Emerson, Hatton et al. 2011)), and the organisations which provide care services.

Social Return calculation – how much was it worth?

With nearly £75,000 invested directly in Skills for People Quality Checkers' team, people who buy the audits or who buy the training would like to know what they're getting back. This is usually presented in the form of an SROI Ratio, how much you should expect back in benefits, divided by the amount you spend. Since each individual Quality Checker audit benefits a number of different stakeholder groups, the SROI ratio is based on the total return across all stakeholder groups, divided by the amount invested (which also avoids double-counting any benefits).

As a pie chart in the last section illustrates, some stakeholders definitely have a financial interest, especially those that either spend or receive money and are able to spend the money in other areas (the commissioners and the care providers). The financial interests of some stakeholders may be of less interest to the organisation that actually pays the money. For example: a provider of social care services will be interested in what they get their money, and will be less interested in what the regulators or policy advisors get. None-the-less, there are real and tangible benefits to each stakeholder group, and real and tangible investment in time or payments.

The SROI ratio is worked out as follows:

SROI Ratio (based on investment over the period in scope Apr 2008 - Oct 2010)	Investment	Return
Total Investment (QC, support time, training, etc)	£ 256,583	
Total Benefits (Social Return, 5 years NPV)		£ 2,927,102
SROI Ratio		11.41

This calculation illustrates that, for every £1000 invested in all aspects of Quality Checker audits (ie the costs of the audits themselves, support staff, QC training, people's own time to attend training, etc), on average the person paying the money should expect to see the equivalent of around £11,410 worth of benefits in return. A commissioning organisation might see a little less whilst providers also benefited. But if a provider were to pay for Quality Checker audits, then the commissioner would gain benefits for free. So the average is correct overall.

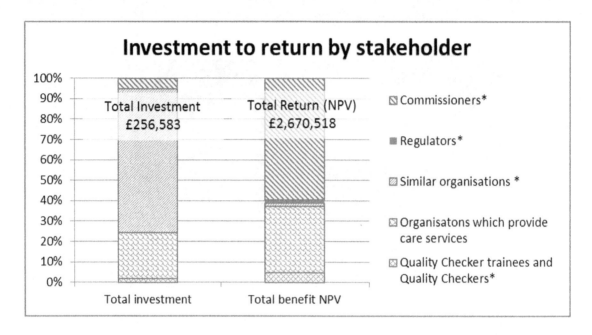

The ratio is different for different organisations, since some invested heavily in training Quality Checkers but do not have any way to recover any direct financial benefit back as the Quality Checkers themselves receive the fees for the audits.

Note that the total amount recorded as spent on Quality Checker audits includes the money an organisation spent on travel and support for their own Quality Checkers (eg for attending training, meeting to discuss audits, networking and so on), even though very few of the Quality Checker teams around the country (apart from Skills for People) are actively performing audits. Once they reach the point of performing audits, then the total value of the benefits should increase. This means the ratio is a little bit of an underestimate. This does not form part of the sensitivity analysis because the amount of impact could not be quantified.

Sensitivity analysis: how accurate are these numbers?

The stakeholders together with the investigator were very careful to make sure that each of the numbers listed above is as reliable as possible. We've challenged each other to make sure that we have the right numbers, and reviewed carefully. We've compared numbers calculated from different organisations, and we've allowed other organisations to look at them and say whether they think the numbers are reasonable or not. They are pretty good.

But we always want to explore all possible options. Based on the calculations we used, I could see what was different between different providers, and I could compare what the very best result, and what the very worst result, might look like.

I've put these in a sensitivity table with the impact map. Here are some examples, though the possible outcomes are summarised in the chart below.

- If we decided that we do have enough evidence to include the 6 people who had challenging behaviour (annual cost to support £133,333 per year each) before Quality Checker audits and none afterwards, this would change the Present Value over 5 years to Commissioners of this section from £1,394,287 to £3,133,210. Over the whole study, this would change the SROI ratio to 18.19.

- If we ignore that and assume that the cost of supporting someone with "frustrated" behaviour is not the average, but the lowest of the costs submitted by organisations, then the Present Value to Commissioners of this section would change from £1,394,287 to £688,208, and the SROI ratio would change to 8.66

Taking all of the sensitivities from the Impact Map together, we get the range of SROI ratios as follows:

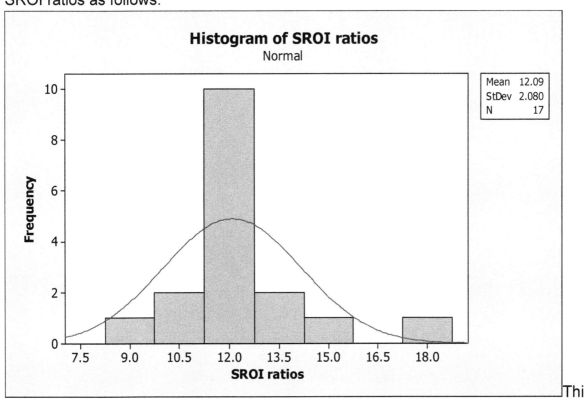

This gives us an average SROI ratio close to 12 which is very similar to the base SROI ratio of 11.41.

Quality Checker audits are relatively low cost and high impact. The Quality Checkers would expect to repeat an audit on each service every 2 years or up to every 5 years, and the audits themselves are low cost, which means that all of the faults that are costing money accumulate during the period between audits. Therefore this relatively high ratio of cost-benefit is to be expected.

Stakeholders identified but not included

We identified the key stakeholder groups, and I confirmed this with other people familiar with social care and with adults with learning disabilities. For each of those stakeholder groups, Skills for People and I jointly identified everyone they could think of. We then made contact with all of them, and attempted to involve them in providing information to the preparation of this report. We also recognised that additional people might be identified by the people we interviewed. The main criterion was to have a minimum of two people (and preferably people representing at least 3 organisations) representing each stakeholder group.

Inevitably, some people selected themselves out by not being contactable. On the whole, we managed to pursue the most appropriate people from organisation to organisation and speak with them, but it was not always possible. I wanted to make sure that I had interviews from people with a range of views about the benefits that the Quality Checkers might deliver, both negative and positive.

Out of 55 people whose names I accumulated over the course of the interviews, 36 people were interviewed, including two in groups of three. Some managed only a single interview, but 10 managed two or more interviews. In addition to the 55, I interviewed a group who had received a Quality Checker audits; there were five people in the group.

Independently of this evaluation, a number of people suggested that friends and family are an important stakeholder group. I discussed this with the Quality Checkers and with staff directly involved with people who receive audits. The inclusion of these groups raises some important issues, and the general feeling was that an approach to friends and family would directly contradict the independent status of the people receiving support.

There were three sets of stakeholders in this group, and the reason for their exclusion is given below each set:

1. **Friends and family of people receiving checks**

Most people live full and active lives, and people receiving support to live independent lives may be involved in many projects, clubs, activities and schemes through the year and at any one time. People (like you or I) would not always discuss their activities with friends or family, when they see them at social occasions; and they might not be able to compare "before" and "after" – particularly this long after the audits took place

2. Friends and family of people doing the checks (the Quality Checkers)

Are unlikely to discuss the minutiae of their jobs, or the questionnaires or surveys in a social context – in the same way that you and I don't discuss these with friends and family. In most cases Quality Checker friends and family would not know what a Quality Checker is.

3. Friends and family of people receiving training

A combination of both of the above: friends and family want to talk about social activities and plan their joint activities, not question whether their independent friend is getting the support to be independent – that is the responsibility of the person.

To test these hypotheses, I approached family members of two active Quality Checkers, speaking eventually to one family member for each Quality Checker.

These two people broadly agreed with the reasons given above. Both of them knew what Quality Checkers do, but confirmed that their independent sister/ son was under no obligation to speak to them about Quality Checkers, and took care to keep confidential or privileged information confidential.

These relatives raised a number of important points that the Quality Checkers themselves were in no position to raise, about the difference it made to the lives of the Quality Checkers themselves, so I have added their comments in to the section on Quality Checker trainees and Quality Checkers. In the light of a strong recommendation from organisations and from individuals, I feel it would be counter-productive for me to assign a value to the feelings of family and friends uni-laterally.

Some key organisations, e.g. Care Quality Commission (CQC), were difficult to speak to, but persistence paid off. I achieved my intention to interview a number of stakeholders in each stakeholder group, in order to be able to triangulate their results.

Outcomes identified but not included, for each stakeholder, and the rationale

All of the outcomes identified by each stakeholder were recorded from the interview record, and the person interviewed make corrections to that interview record, when they received it.

Those outcomes have been recorded in the Impact Map and the text, both positive and negative.

Any financial proxies not included, and the rationale

In some cases, the stakeholders and other people asked were strongly opposed to assigning a financial equivalence value. Examples include "Community Involvement" and "Contributing to the community by voting" (both of the stakeholder group People who received audits), where the financial equivalents in the literature were considered simply wrong.

In other cases, one stakeholder may have identified a financial equivalent to their benefit when other stakeholders in the same stakeholder group were not able to assign a financial equivalence value. I discussed this with the stakeholders, both the one who had identified the financial benefit, and the ones who had identified the same benefit but not financial equivalent, and we agreed an appropriate way to report the information. In many cases, once one organisation had estimated the value of a benefit and given their rationale for doing so, other organisations were able to access the same information in their records and provide their own financial value to the benefit that they had identified.

Some stakeholders used additional information to estimate their own benefits in terms of the financial equivalent. Other stakeholders were not able to do this. All financial equivalents have only been applied to those stakeholders who confirmed that they had received that amount of benefit. Those stakeholders who did not feel able to accept the financial equivalent have not had the value added. This means that the figures are as conservative as they can be, and reflect what stakeholders are comfortable with.

Documents referred to

Alleyne, R. (2009). Loneliness as harmful as smoking and obesity, say scientists. The Telegraph. London.

Bradley, G. and Stationery Office (2010). Fundamentals of Benefits Realisation, The Stationary Office.

Communities & Local Government (2011). Local authority revenue expenditure and financing England: 2010-11 Budget (revised). London, Communities & Local Government.

DH (2009). Valuing People Now: a new three-year strategy for people with learning disabilities. D. o. Health, HM Government: v, 143.

DH (2009). Valuing People Now: Impact Assessment. D. o. Health. London, HM Government: 38.

Emerson, E., C. Hatton, J. Robertson, H. Roberts, S. Baines and G. Glover (2011). People with Learning Disabilities in England 2010: Services & Supports. Durham, Improving Health and Lives (IHAL)

Learning Disabilities Observatory: 71.

Emler, N. (2001). Self-esteem: the costs and causes of low self-worth. York, UK, Joseph Rowntree Foundation: vi, 98.

Findlay, R. A. (2003). "Interventions to reduce social isolation amongst older people: where is the evidence?" Ageing & Society 23: 647-658.

Findlay, R. A. and C. Cartwright (2002). Social Isolation & Older People: A Literature Review. Queensland, Australia, Australasian Centre on Ageing, the University of Queensland: 28.

Fyson, R., B. Tarieton and L. Ward (2007). The impact of the Supporting People programme on adults with learning disabilities. York, Joseph Rowntree Foundation: 4.

Heywood, F. (2001). Money well spent: the effectiveness and value of housing adaptations. P. Press and J. R. Foundation.

Hirsch, D. (2008). Estimating the costs of child poverty. York, Joseph Rowntree Foundation: 12.

Kegan, D. (1978). "The Quality of Student Life and Financial Costs: The Cost of Social Isolation." Journal of College Student Personnel January 1978: 55-58.

Kilsby, M. and S. Beyer (2010). A Financial Cost:Benefit Analysis of Kent Supported Employment - Establishing a Framework for Analysis (An Interim Report), Kent County Council: 31.

Lewis, R. Q., R. Rosen, N. Goodwin and J. Dixon (2010). Where next for integrated care organisations in the English NHS? London, UK, King's Fund

Nuffield Trust: 44.

Lovell, C. (2008, 28 March 2008). "Health inspectorate finds progress for Cornwall Trust." Community Care Retrieved 25 nov 2010, 2010.

Michael, S. J. (2008). Healthcare for All: Independent INQUIRY into access to healthcare for people with learning disabilities. London, NHS: 72.

Snell, J. (2007). Cornwall learning disabilities scandal: has the tide turned? Community Care, Community Care. **2010**.

Stein, M. (2006). "Research Review: Young people leaving care." Child and Family Social WOrk **11**(3): 273-279.

Surowiecki, J. (2005). The wisdom of crowds : why the many are smarter than the few. London, Abacus.

Thomas, C. and S. Morris (2003). "Cost of Depression amongst Adults in England in 2000." British Journal of Psychiatry **183**: 514-519.

Treasury, H. (2003). The Green Book - Appraisal and Evaluation in Central Government, HM Treasury.

Turnbull, J. C. (2006). Turnbull Judgement. Housing and council tax benefits. Sheffield.

Worcs Reach Review Team (2009). Reach Review in Worcestershire - what we found out. Worcester, UK, Worcestershire Supporting People Partnership: 29.

Worcs SP team (2010). Financial Benefits of Supporting People in Worcestershire. Worcester, UK, Worcestershire Supporting People Partnership: 25.

Zappalà, G. and M. Lyons (2010). Recent approaches to measuring social impact in the third sector: an overview. Knowledge Connect - connecting you to social impact thinking worldwide, The Centre for Social Impact (Australia).